These
Sermon Notes
Belong to

. . . .

© 2012 by Barbour Publishing, Inc.

ISBNs 978-1-64352-011-7; 978-1-64352-012-4

All scripture quotations are taken from the King James Version of the Bible.

Published by Barbour Books, an imprint of Barbour Publishing, Inc., 1810 Barbour Drive, Uhrichsville, Ohio 44683, www.barbourbooks.com

Our mission is to inspire the world with the life-changing message of the Bible.

 Member of the
Evangelical Christian
Publishers Association

Printed in China.

Sermon Notes

BARBOUR BOOKS
An Imprint of Barbour Publishing, Inc.

Let us seek to be useful.
Let us seek to be vessels fit for the Master's use,
that God, the Holy Spirit, may shine fully through us.

D. L. MOODY

Title/Topic:

Speaker:

Date:

Key scriptures:

Notes:

The main point:

> My friends, it is one thing to go to church or chapel;
> it is quite another thing to go to God.
>
> CHARLES SPURGEON

Title/Topic: ....

Speaker: ....

Date: ....

Key scriptures: ....

Notes: ....

....

....

....

....

....

....

....

....

....

....

....

....

....

....

The main point:

One of the greatest truths of the Bible
is that God loves us. And because He loves us,
He wants to give us what is best for us.

BILLY GRAHAM

Title/Topic:

Speaker:

Date:

Key scriptures:

Notes:

The main point:

I will lift up mine eyes unto the hills,
from whence cometh my help. My help cometh
*from the L*ORD*, which made heaven and earth.*

PSALM 121:1–2

Title/Topic: ....

Speaker: ....

Date: ....

Key scriptures: ....

Notes: ....

....

....

....

....

....

....

....

....

....

....

....

....

....

....

The main point:

> Don't measure the size of the mountain;
> talk to the One who can move it.
>
> Max Lucado

Title/Topic: ....

Speaker: ....

Date: ....

Key scriptures: ....

Notes: ....

....

....

....

....

....

....

....

....

....

....

....

....

....

....

....

....

The main point:

> Faith is the hand by which my soul touches God.
> BILLY SUNDAY

Title/Topic: ....

Speaker: ....

Date: ....

Key scriptures: ....

Notes: ....

....

....

....

....

....

....

....

....

....

....

....

....

....

....

....

....

....

The main point:

Love to God is obedience, love to God is holiness.
To love God and to love man is to be conformed
to the image of Christ; and this is salvation.

CHARLES SPURGEON

Title/Topic: ....

Speaker: ....

Date: ....

Key scriptures: ....

Notes: ....

....

....

....

....

....

....

....

....

....

....

....

....

....

....

....

The main point:

> Heaven is filled with a company
> of those who have been twice born.
>
> D. L. MOODY

Title/Topic: ....

Speaker: ....

Date: ....

Key scriptures: ....

Notes: ....

....

....

....

....

....

....

....

....

....

....

....

....

....

....

The main point:

The things which are impossible
with men are possible with God.
LUKE 18:27

Title/Topic: ....

Speaker: ....

Date: ....

Key scriptures: ....

Notes: ....

....

....

....

....

....

....

....

....

....

....

....

....

....

....

The main point:

Hope sees a crown in reserve, mansions in
readiness, and Jesus Himself preparing a place
for us, and by the rapturous sight she sustains
the soul under the sorrows of the hour.

CHARLES SPURGEON

Title/Topic: ....

Speaker: ....

Date: ....

Key scriptures: ....

Notes: ....

....

....

....

....

....

....

....

....

....

....

....

....

....

....

....

The main point:

Faith is not believing just anything;
it is believing God.
E. M. BOUNDS

Title/Topic: ....

Speaker: ....

Date: ....

Key scriptures: ....

Notes: ....

....

....

....

....

....

....

....

....

....

....

....

....

....

....

....

The main point:

No matter who you are or what your life has been
like so far, the rest of your life's journey can be different.
With God's help you can begin again.

BILLY GRAHAM

Title/Topic: ....

Speaker: ....

Date: ....

Key scriptures: ....

Notes: ....

....

....

....

....

....

....

....

....

....

....

....

....

....

....

The main point:

> If I am adopted, I have become a child;
> God is no longer my judge but my Father.
>
> D. L. MOODY

Title/Topic: ....

Speaker: ....

Date: ....

Key scriptures: ....

Notes: ....

....

....

....

....

....

....

....

....

....

....

....

....

....

....

The main point:

Jesus Christ the same yesterday,
and to day, and for ever.
HEBREWS 13:8

Title/Topic:

Speaker:

Date:

Key scriptures:

Notes:

The main point:

God's children are God's children anywhere and
everywhere, and shall be even unto the end. Nothing
can sever that sacred tie or divide us from His heart.

CHARLES SPURGEON

Title/Topic: ....

Speaker: ....

Date: ....

Key scriptures: ....

Notes: ....

....

....

....

....

....

....

....

....

....

....

....

....

....

....

The main point:

God has an individual plan for each person.
If you will go to Him and submit to Him,
He will come into your heart and commune with you.

JOYCE MEYER

Title/Topic: ....

Speaker: ....

Date: ....

Key scriptures: ....

Notes: ....

....

....

....

....

....

....

....

....

....

....

....

....

....

....

....

The main point:

> God will not let you go.
> Max Lucado

Title/Topic: ....

Speaker: ....

Date: ....

Key scriptures: ....

Notes: ....

....

....

....

....

....

....

....

....

....

....

....

....

....

....

....

The main point:

> We cannot be lukewarm;
> we have to be on fire with the cause of Christ.
> D. L. MOODY

Title/Topic: ....

Speaker: ....

Date: ....

Key scriptures: ....

Notes: ....

....

....

....

....

....

....

....

....

....

....

....

....

....

....

....

The main point:

And whatsoever ye do, do it heartily,
as to the Lord, and not unto men.
COLOSSIANS 3:23

Title/Topic: ....

Speaker: ....

Date: ....

Key scriptures: ....

Notes: ....

....

....

....

....

....

....

....

....

....

....

....

....

....

....

....

The main point:

> Who can describe the tokens of God's goodness that
> are extended to the human race even in this life?
>
> AUGUSTINE

Title/Topic: ....

Speaker: ....

Date: ....

Key scriptures: ....

Notes: ....

....

....

....

....

....

....

....

....

....

....

....

....

....

The main point:

Keep your life so constant in its contact with God
that His surprising power may break out on the right hand
and on the left. Always be in a state of expectancy, and see
that you leave room for God to come in as He likes.

OSWALD CHAMBERS

Title/Topic: ....

Speaker: ....

Date: ....

Key scriptures: ....

Notes: ....

....

....

....

....

....

....

....

....

....

....

....

....

....

....

The main point:

When God dwells at the center of our lives,
peace and contentment will belong to us
just as surely as we belong to God.

BETH MOORE

Title/Topic: ....

Speaker: ....

Date: ....

Key scriptures: ....

Notes: ....

....

....

....

....

....

....

....

....

....

....

....

....

....

....

....

The main point:

> I would a thousand times rather that
> God's will should be done than my own.
>
> D. L. MOODY

Title/Topic: ....

Speaker: ....

Date: ....

Key scriptures: ....

Notes: ....

....

....

....

....

....

....

....

....

....

....

....

....

....

....

....

The main point:

This is the day which the LORD hath made;
we will rejoice and be glad in it.

PSALM 118:24

Title/Topic:

Speaker:

Date:

Key scriptures:

Notes:

The main point:

God has forgiven us continuously. He not only forgave
us at the first all our sins, but He continues daily to forgive,
for the act of forgiveness is a continuous one.

CHARLES SPURGEON

Title/Topic: ....

Speaker: ....

Date: ....

Key scriptures: ....

Notes: ....

....

....

....

....

....

....

....

....

....

....

....

....

....

....

The main point:

> If God can make a billion galaxies, can't He make
> good out of our bad and sense out of our faltering lives?
> Of course He can. He is God.
>
> MAX LUCADO

Title/Topic: ....

Speaker: ....

Date: ....

Key scriptures: ....

Notes: ....

....

....

....

....

....

....

....

....

....

....

....

....

....

....

The main point:

> What has Jesus Christ ever asked you
> to do that wasn't for your own good?
> BILLY SUNDAY

Title/Topic: ....

Speaker: ....

Date: ....

Key scriptures: ....

Notes: ....

....

....

....

....

....

....

....

....

....

....

....

....

....

....

....

The main point:

When Christ cried out on Calvary, "It is finished!"
He meant what He said. All that men have to do now
is just accept the work of Jesus Christ.
D. L. MOODY

Title/Topic: ....

Speaker: ....

Date: ....

Key scriptures: ....

Notes: ....

....

....

....

....

....

....

....

....

....

....

....

....

....

....

....

The main point:

Turn us again, O God, and cause thy
face to shine; and we shall be saved.
PSALM 80:3

Title/Topic:

Speaker:

Date:

Key scriptures:

Notes:

The main point:

> Grace is something not which I improve,
> but which improves, employs me, works on me.
> CHARLES SPURGEON

Title/Topic: ....

Speaker: ....

Date: ....

Key scriptures: ....

Notes: ....

....

....

....

....

....

....

....

....

....

....

....

....

....

....

The main point:

I don't want any of those things I fear to happen,
but this I know, if they do, my God will take
care of me, my God will take care of me!

BETH MOORE

Title/Topic: ....

Speaker: ....

Date: ....

Key scriptures: ....

Notes: ....

....

....

....

....

....

....

....

....

....

....

....

....

....

....

The main point:

> Focusing intently on Christ naturally results
> in a lifestyle of greater and greater selflessness.
> CHARLES SWINDOLL

Title/Topic: ....

Speaker: ....

Date: ....

Key scriptures: ....

Notes: ....

....

....

....

....

....

....

....

....

....

....

....

....

....

....

....

The main point:

> Some people think God does not like to be
> troubled with our constant coming and asking.
> The only way to trouble God is not to come at all.
>
> D. L. MOODY

Title/Topic: ....

Speaker: ....

Date: ....

Key scriptures: ....

Notes: ....

....

....

....

....

....

....

....

....

....

....

....

....

....

....

....

The main point:

Behold, God is my salvation; I will trust, and not
*be afraid: for the L*ORD *J*EHOVAH *is my strength*
and my song; he also is become my salvation.

ISAIAH 12:2

Title/Topic:

Speaker:

Date:

Key scriptures:

Notes:

The main point:

Hear this, and be astonished: He can create you a
second time; He can cause you to be born again. This is
a miracle of grace, but the Holy Ghost will perform it.
CHARLES SPURGEON

Title/Topic: ....

Speaker: ....

Date: ....

Key scriptures: ....

Notes: ....

....

....

....

....

....

....

....

....

....

....

....

....

....

....

The main point:

> There is no way to travel from the state of sinfulness to
> the state of holiness except by the highway of grace.
> JOYCE MEYER

Title/Topic: ....

Speaker: ....

Date: ....

Key scriptures: ....

Notes: ....

....

....

....

....

....

....

....

....

....

....

....

....

....

....

....

The main point:

It is an honor to believe what the lips of Jesus taught.
I had sooner be a fool with Christ than a
wise man with the philosophers.

CHARLES SPURGEON

Title/Topic: ....

Speaker: ....

Date: ....

Key scriptures: ....

Notes: ....

....

....

....

....

....

....

....

....

....

....

....

....

....

....

....

The main point:

> If God says it, let us take our stand upon it.
> D. L. MOODY

Title/Topic: ....

Speaker: ....

Date: ....

Key scriptures: ....

Notes: ....

....

....

....

....

....

....

....

....

....

....

....

....

....

....

The main point:

Wisdom is the principal thing; therefore get wisdom:
and with all thy getting get understanding.
PROVERBS 4:7

Title/Topic: ....

Speaker: ....

Date: ....

Key scriptures: ....

Notes: ....

....

....

....

....

....

....

....

....

....

....

....

....

....

....

....

The main point:

> Our Lord Jesus did not die for imaginary sins,
> but His heart's blood was spilt to wash out deep
> crimson stains, which nothing else can remove.
>
> CHARLES SPURGEON

Title/Topic: ....

Speaker: ....

Date: ....

Key scriptures: ....

Notes: ....

....

....

....

....

....

....

....

....

....

....

....

....

....

....

The main point:

> All around us are people who are lost and
> separated from their heavenly Father, and we
> have a responsibility to tell them about Him.
> BILLY GRAHAM

Title/Topic: ....

Speaker: ....

Date: ....

Key scriptures: ....

Notes: ....

....

....

....

....

....

....

....

....

....

....

....

....

....

....

The main point:

> For grace is given not because we have done good works,
> but in order that we may be able to do them.
>
> AUGUSTINE

Title/Topic: ....

Speaker: ....

Date: ....

Key scriptures: ....

Notes: ....

....

....

....

....

....

....

....

....

....

....

....

....

....

....

....

The main point:

> You might say the whole plan of salvation is in
> two words—Giving; Receiving. God gives; I receive.
> D. L. MOODY

Title/Topic: ....

Speaker: ....

Date: ....

Key scriptures: ....

Notes: ....

....

....

....

....

....

....

....

....

....

....

....

....

....

....

The main point:

Now faith is the substance of things hoped for,
the evidence of things not seen.
HEBREWS 11:1

Title/Topic: ....

Speaker: ....

Date: ....

Key scriptures: ....

Notes: ....

....

....

....

....

....

....

....

....

....

....

....

....

....

....

....

The main point:

> What is heaven but to be with God, to dwell with Him,
> to realize that God is mine, and I am His?
>
> CHARLES SPURGEON

Title/Topic: ....

Speaker: ....

Date: ....

Key scriptures: ....

Notes: ....

....

....

....

....

....

....

....

....

....

....

....

....

....

....

....

The main point:

> Jesus could not pay the price for our sin by hiding
> in the safety of the upper room, and we cannot
> remain in the safety of the sanctuary.
>
> CHARLES SWINDOLL

Title/Topic:

Speaker:

Date:

Key scriptures:

Notes:

The main point:

Exhibit God with your uniqueness. When you magnify
your Maker with your strengths, when your contribution
enriches God's reputation, your days grow suddenly sweet.
MAX LUCADO

Title/Topic: ....

Speaker: ....

Date: ....

Key scriptures: ....

Notes: ....

....

....

....

....

....

....

....

....

....

....

....

....

....

....

....

The main point:

It seems to me that if we get one look at Christ
in His love and beauty, this world and its
pleasures will look very small to us.

D. L. MOODY

Title/Topic: ....

Speaker: ....

Date: ....

Key scriptures: ....

Notes: ....

....

....

....

....

....

....

....

....

....

....

....

....

....

....

The main point:

Looking unto Jesus the author and finisher of our faith; who for the joy that was set before him endured the cross, despising the shame, and is set down at the right hand of the throne of God.

HEBREWS 12:2

Title/Topic:

Speaker:

Date:

Key scriptures:

Notes:

The main point:

There is no place like Calvary for creating confidence.
The air of that sacred hill brings health to trembling faith.

CHARLES SPURGEON

Title/Topic: ....

Speaker: ....

Date: ....

Key scriptures: ....

Notes: ....

....

....

....

....

....

....

....

....

....

....

....

....

....

....

The main point:

> Sometimes we get tired of the burdens of life,
> but we know that Jesus Christ will meet us at the end
> of our life's journey—and that makes all the difference.
> BILLY GRAHAM

Title/Topic: ....

Speaker: ....

Date: ....

Key scriptures: ....

Notes: ....

....

....

....

....

....

....

....

....

....

....

....

....

....

....

....

The main point:

> We must not trust every saying or suggestion,
> but warily and patiently ponder things
> according to the will of God.
>
> THOMAS À KEMPIS

Title/Topic: ....

Speaker: ....

Date: ....

Key scriptures: ....

Notes: ....

....

....

....

....

....

....

....

....

....

....

....

....

....

....

....

The main point:

> If there is a cry coming up from a heart broken
> on account of sin, God will hear that cry.
>
> D. L. MOODY

Title/Topic: ....

Speaker: ....

Date: ....

Key scriptures: ....

Notes: ....

....

....

....

....

....

....

....

....

....

....

....

....

....

....

....

The main point:

The LORD is my light and my salvation;
whom shall I fear? the LORD is the strength
of my life; of whom shall I be afraid?

PSALM 27:1

Title/Topic: ....

Speaker: ....

Date: ....

Key scriptures: ....

Notes: ....

....

....

....

....

....

....

....

....

....

....

....

....

....

....

The main point:

> The Christian life was intended not to be a sitting still,
> but a race, a perpetual motion.
>
> CHARLES SPURGEON

Title/Topic: ....

Speaker: ....

Date: ....

Key scriptures: ....

Notes: ....

....

....

....

....

....

....

....

....

....

....

....

....

....

....

....

The main point:

> Our blessings include life and health, family and friends,
> freedom and possessions...the gifts we receive from
> God are multiplied when we share them.
>
> BETH MOORE

Title/Topic:

Speaker:

Date:

Key scriptures:

Notes:

The main point:

> What is needed today is not a new gospel, but live men
> and women who can re-state the Gospel of the Son of God
> in terms that will reach the very heart of our problems.
> OSWALD CHAMBERS

Title/Topic: ....

Speaker: ....

Date: ....

Key scriptures: ....

Notes: ....

....

....

....

....

....

....

....

....

....

....

....

....

....

....

....

The main point:

> He only is safe for eternity who is sheltered
> behind the finished work of Christ.
> D. L. MOODY

Title/Topic: ....

Speaker: ....

Date: ....

Key scriptures: ....

Notes: ....

....

....

....

....

....

....

....

....

....

....

....

....

....

....

....

The main point:

And the peace of God, which passeth all understanding,
shall keep your hearts and minds through Christ Jesus.
PHILIPPIANS 4:7

Title/Topic:

Speaker:

Date:

Key scriptures:

Notes:

The main point:

Blessed Bible! thou art all truth.

<small>Charles Spurgeon</small>

Title/Topic: ....

Speaker: ....

Date: ....

Key scriptures: ....

Notes: ....

....

....

....

....

....

....

....

....

....

....

....

....

....

....

....

....

The main point:

> Some convert the lost. Some encourage the saved.
> And some keep the movement going. All are needed.
>
> MAX LUCADO

Title/Topic: ....

Speaker: ....

Date: ....

Key scriptures: ....

Notes: ....

....

....

....

....

....

....

....

....

....

....

....

....

....

....

....

The main point:

> God did not give us His Word to satisfy
> our curiosity but to change our lives.
> CHARLES SWINDOLL

Title/Topic: ....

Speaker: ....

Date: ....

Key scriptures: ....

Notes: ....

....

....

....

....

....

....

....

....

....

....

....

....

....

....

....

The main point:

> It is a great mistake to be looking at obstacles
> when we have such a God to look at.
>
> D. L. MOODY

Title/Topic:

Speaker:

Date:

Key scriptures:

Notes:

The main point:

*Trust in the LORD with all thine heart; and lean not
unto thine own understanding. In all thy ways
acknowledge him, and he shall direct thy paths.*

PROVERBS 3:5-6

Title/Topic: ....

Speaker: ....

Date: ....

Key scriptures: ....

Notes: ....

....

....

....

....

....

....

....

....

....

....

....

....

....

....

....

The main point:

> If anything has been accomplished through my life,
> it has been solely God's doing, not mine,
> and He—not I—must get the credit.
>
> BILLY GRAHAM

Title/Topic:

Speaker:

Date:

Key scriptures:

Notes:

The main point:

> When Christ becomes our central focus, contentment
> replaces our anxiety as well as our fears and insecurities.
>
> CHARLES SWINDOLL

Title/Topic: ....

Speaker: ....

Date: ....

Key scriptures: ....

Notes: ....

....

....

....

....

....

....

....

....

....

....

....

....

....

....

The main point:

> **Faith is believing right here with your
> head no matter how your heart feels.**
> BETH MOORE

Title/Topic: ....

Speaker: ....

Date: ....

Key scriptures: ....

Notes: ....

....

....

....

....

....

....

....

....

....

....

....

....

....

....

....

....

The main point:

You will never have true pleasure or peace
or joy or comfort until you have found Christ.
D. L. MOODY

Title/Topic: ....

Speaker: ....

Date: ....

Key scriptures: ....

Notes: ....

....

....

....

....

....

....

....

....

....

....

....

....

....

....

....

The main point:

For where your treasure is,
there will your heart be also.

MATTHEW 6:21

Title/Topic:

Speaker:

Date:

Key scriptures:

Notes:

The main point:

He knew me before I knew myself;
yea, He knew me before I was myself.

CHARLES SPURGEON

Title/Topic: ....

Speaker: ....

Date: ....

Key scriptures: ....

Notes: ....

....

....

....

....

....

....

....

....

....

....

....

....

....

The main point:

THE TIME-TESTED KING JAMES VERSION OF SCRIPTURE IS THE PERFECT COMPANION!

KJV Deluxe Gift & Award Bible

This award Bible, featuring the complete text of the King James
Version, makes an ideal presentation for commencements, Vacation Bible
Schools, Sunday school graduations, and other gift-giving occasions.
Featuring the words of Christ in red, a dictionary and concordance,
Bible books-at-a-glance, annual Bible reading plan, time line, maps, and more,
this *KJV Deluxe Gift & Award Bible* is appropriate for all readers.

DiCarta / 978-1-63409-074-2 / $14.99